FAST BREAKS

and

FANATICS

Behind the Scenes
of Game Day Basketball

by Martin Driscoll

CAPSTONE PRESS
a capstone imprint

Published by Spark, an imprint of Capstone
1710 Roe Crest Drive, North Mankato, Minnesota 56003
capstonepub.com

Library of Congress Cataloging-in-Publication Data is available on the Library of Congress website.

ISBN: 9781669003335 (hardcover)
ISBN: 9781669040279 (paperback)
ISBN: 9781669003298 (ebook PDF)

Summary: Think pro basketball begins with the opening tip-off? Think again! In this Sports Illustrated Kids book, go behind the scenes of a typical game day in professional basketball—from cleaning the hardcourt and mascot madness to locker-room pep talks and postgame interviews. This fast-paced, fact-filled book will give basketball fans of all ages a totally fresh perspective on big-time basketball.

Editorial Credits
Editor: Donald Lemke; Designer: Tracy Davies; Media Researcher: Svetlana Zhurkin; Production Specialist: Katy LaVigne

Image Credits
Associated Press: Ashley Landis, 17; Getty Images: AFP/Timothy A. Clary, 12, Alika Jenner, 19, Allen Berezovsky, 18, Claus Andersen, 27, Elsa, 23, Ezra Shaw, 26, Hannah Foslien, 16, Jonathan Daniel, 25, NBAE/Bill Baptist, 22, NBAE/David Dow, 9, NBAE/David Sherman, 7, 10, NBAE/Garrett Ellwood, 20, NBAE/Jim Poorten, 21, NBAE/Joe Murphy, 6, NBAE/Kate Frese, 15, NBAE/Nathaniel S. Butler, 11, NBAE/Rocky Widner, 13, Otto Greule Jr., 24, Sports Illustrated/John W. McDonough, 14, The Denver Post/John Leyba, 8; Shutterstock: Alex Kravtsov, cover (top back and bottom left), elisa galceran garcia, 29 (top), M. Budniak, 29 (bottom), niwat chaiyawoo, cover (top right), 1, popular.vector, 29 (basketball icon), Rawpixel, cover (bottom right), Ron Alvey, cover (bottom middle), Ron Dale (background), cover, back cover, WoodysPhotos, 28; Sports Illustrated: Erick W. Rasco, 4, 5

Printed and bound in the USA. 5195

TABLE OF CONTENTS

Words in **bold** are in the glossary.

HOOP IT UP

Two basketball teams head onto the court. Players stretch and take warm-up shots. Balls clank off the rim or swish through the net. Soon the game will begin.

LeBron James

The WNBA's New York Liberty play against the Connecticut Sun.

Fans have come to watch the best players in the world. The sport's biggest stars play in the National Basketball Association (NBA) and the Women's National Basketball Association (WNBA).

GETTING READY

Each team has a **shootaround** on game day. These practices are often in the morning. Coaches explain their plan to beat their **opponent**. Players practice shots they are likely to take in the game.

Members of the Minnesota Timberwolves during a shootaround

The shootaround lasts for about an hour.

Afterward, players have time to eat and rest.

FACT ///

The shootaround was the idea of NBA coach Bill Sharman. He coached the Los Angeles Lakers in the 1970s.

Team trainers have an important job.
Their goal is to keep players healthy. If players
get hurt, trainers help them heal.

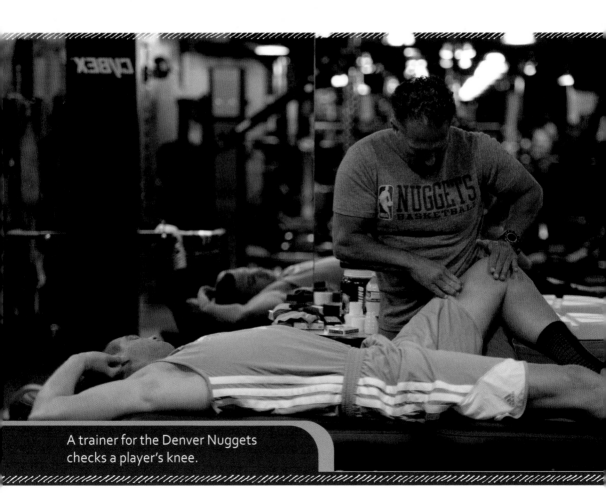

A trainer for the Denver Nuggets checks a player's knee.

A trainer for the Phoenix Mercury tapes player Penny Taylor's ankle.

The training room gets busy before game time. Players hurry in for help with sore muscles and joints. Trainers tape ankles. They stretch and massage stiff muscles.

Minnesota Lynx locker room

A WNBA or NBA locker room is a home away from home. Each player has space for uniforms, shoes, and equipment. Many lockers also have video screens or music players.

Before each game, a team meeting takes place in the locker room. Coaches speak to players. They explain their **strategy** for the game. Then players head to the court.

GAME TIME

Loud music booms through the arena. The lights over the court go dim. Then spotlights glare. The crowd cheers. It's time for the starting lineups to be introduced.

LeBron James is a starter for the Los Angeles Lakers.

The **public address announcer** calls the name of each starter. Fans cheer for the home team's starting five.

A jump ball during a game between the Los Angeles Lakers and the Chicago Bulls

The game starts with a jump ball. One player from each team stands at center court. An official tosses the ball into the air. The two players leap for it. They both hope to tap the ball to a teammate.

The crowd cheers when the home team wins the **tip-off**!

The opening tip-off between the
Phoenix Mercury and the Washington Mystics

Three officials are on the court for every NBA and WNBA game. Before the game, the officials make sure the baskets and backboards are set up correctly.

They even check the basketballs. Game balls must be **inflated** perfectly.

ACTION PACKED

The point guard dribbles the ball up the court. He sees a teammate open near the 3-point line. The point guard delivers a perfect pass. His teammate catches it and shoots.

The ball swishes through the net. A referee lifts both arms into the air. It's three points for the home team!

Many fans watch the game on TV.
Broadcasters describe the action for fans at home. They work at a courtside table. They give details about the players and the teams.

In the press box, other members of the **media** are at work. They cover the game for radio, newspapers, and websites.

At halftime, the teams hurry to their locker rooms. Halftime lasts for 15 minutes. A dance team performs for fans.

Then the mascot puts on a show of its own. Mascots thrill fans with amazing dunks and other tricks.

FACT

At halftime, players get to rest, but coaches have work to do. They talk to the team and explain the strategy for the second half.

Orlando Magic mascot Stuff the Magic Dragon

Time is running short. The score is close. The center catches a pass near the basket. The player dribbles around a defender and leaps toward the hoop.

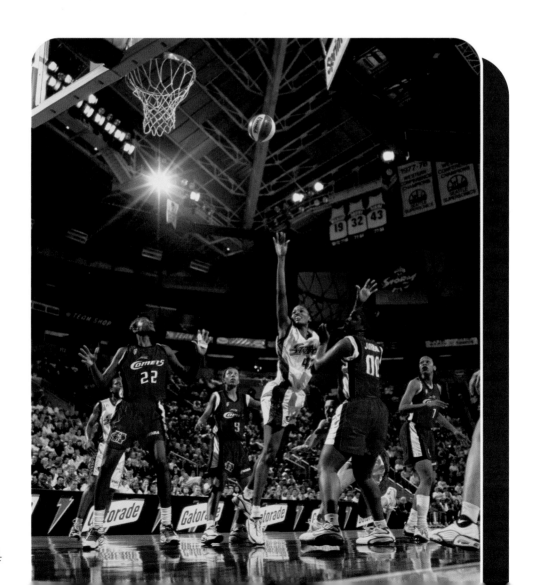

Chicago Bulls forward Tristan Thompson dunks during a game.

A dunk brings the home crowd to its feet. The rim bends under the weight. But it won't break. The rim has springs in it. When the player lets go, it snaps back into place.

FACT

The "breakaway rim" has been used in the NBA for 40 years. It was invented after several backboards shattered during games.

When the home team wins, fans go home happy. But the game day isn't over.

Teams head back to the locker rooms. Coaches and players talk to sports reporters. The reporters ask questions about the game. The answers they get help them explain the game to fans everywhere.

The arena crew has work to do after the game. They sweep the court and clean up around the benches. They also clean up the mess left by thousands of fans.

PLAN YOUR GAME DAY

You can host game day at your house.

- Invite friends over to watch a game.
- Ask an adult to bake some sweet treats.
- Set up a beanbag toss in the basement or backyard. See who can make the longest shot.
- Have chips and dip ready to go. Everyone will want to do some dunking.

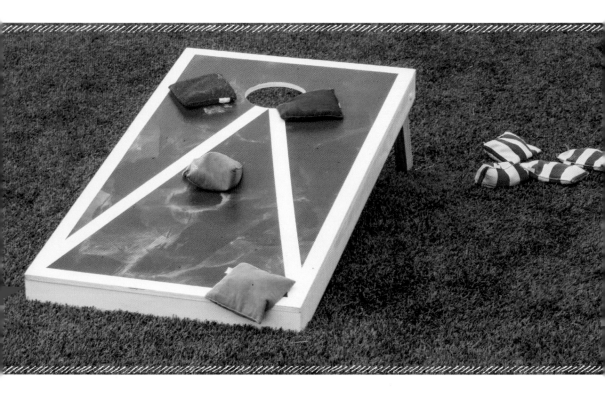

GLOSSARY

broadcaster (BRAHD-kass-tur)—a person who describes the game on television or radio

inflated (in-FLAY-tuhd)—filled with air or gas

media (MEE-dee-uh)—forms of communication or information, such as newspapers, radio, or TV

opponent (uh-POH-nent)—a team that competes against another

public address announcer (PUH-blik UH-drehs uh-NOWN-sur)—a person who uses a loudspeaker system to inform the crowd in an arena

shootaround (SHOOT-uh-rownd)—a relaxed basketball practice session

strategy (STRA-tuh-jee)—a plan to defeat an opponent

tip-off (TIHP-ahf)—putting the ball in play by a jump ball

READ MORE

Allan, John. *Be the Best at Basketball.* Minneapolis: Lerner Books, 2021.

Omoth, Tyler. *Basketball Fun*. North Mankato, MN: Capstone, 2021.

Storden, Thom. *Big-Time Basketball Records*. North Mankato, MN: Capstone, 2022.

INTERNET SITES

Jr. NBA
jr.nba.com

Kiddle: Basketball Facts for Kids
kids.kiddle.co/basketball

Naismith Memorial Basketball Hall of Fame
hoophall.com

INDEX

ABOUT THE AUTHOR

Martin Driscoll is a former newspaper reporter and longtime editor of children's books. He is also the author of several sports books for children, including biographies of legendary stars of boxing, baseball, and basketball. Driscoll lives in southern Minnesota with his wife and two children.